HEALING - THE SHAMAN'S WAY BOOK

CW00919583

Norman W. Wilson PhD

HEALING - THE SHAMAN'S WAY
BOOK 2 - Crystals

ZADKIEL
PUBLISHING

Cover Design by

www.srwalkerdesigns.com

Interior Photography by
Suzanne V. Wilson Photography

DISCLAIMER

There are no guarantees that any of the procedures or suggestions described herein will work. Before following the use of any of these suggestions always consult your medical practitioner. Persons under the age of eighteen should not attempt any of these activities. Please remember you are responsible for how you use the information contained in this book.

Norman W. Wilson, PhD
08/2022

APPRECIATION

I am deeply appreciative of the faith, the help, and the encouragement I have received from each of the following: Stuart Holland, my editor and publisher, Stephen R. Walker for cover design, Omar Lopez for interior graphics and videos, and especially my wife, Suzanne V Wilson for the use of her photos and continued support.

HEALING - THE SHAMAN'S WAY - USING CRYSTALS

CHAPTER ONE
CRYSTALS

INTRODUCTION

Shamanism has been around for thousands of years. The words Shamanism and Shaman are not a part of Native American or First People of Canada languages. The word Shaman was made popular by the late Michael J Harner and his Foundation for Shamanic Studies. In its original language, the Tungus of Siberia, the word Shaman means *one who knows*. The question is: Knows what? A shaman knows what to use and do to help people heal themselves. Modern healers no longer use masks, and dress in animal skins, however, some healers in aboriginal cultures still adorn themselves. Even though the word shaman appears to be masculine a man or woman can be a shaman. In Tungus the word for a woman who is a healer is *shamanka.*

Shamans used what was available in the world of nature: medicines from trees, shrubs, bushes, and plants. That use also included what we now call crystals. For the early cultures, crystals were stones. Some crystal authorities still refer to them as stones. The study of crystals and crystal formation is called crystallography. What then, are crystals? A brief explanation of these three terms, crystals, minerals, and rocks will be helpful.

Crystals are solids:
Crystals are solids that have an organized structure that is, they are homogeneous and have a natural geometrically regular form with symmetrically arranged planes. There are seven crystal systems:

Cubic, Tetragonal, Orthorhombic, Rhombohedral, Hexagonal, Monoclinic and Triclinic

Crystal Systems

FLUROITE		cubic	primitive / body centered / face centered	
ZIRCON		tetragonal	primitive / body centered	
EMERALD		hexagonal		
TANZANITE		orthorhombic	primitive / body centered / face centered / basis face centered	
AZURITE		monoclinic	primitive / basis face centered	
RHODOCHROSITE		trigonal		
AMAZONITE		triclinic		

Crystals are minerals:

A mineral is a naturally occurring inorganic solid, with a definite chemical composition, and an ordered atomic arrangement. All minerals form crystals. Put another way, a crystal is a structure made up of various natural materials; whereas, the mineral is the material itself. It is the internal arrangement of the atoms that determine the chemical, physical properties, and color.

Rocks are divided:

Second is the term rock. According to Petrology, rocks are divided into three major classes. The division is done according to the processes through which the rocks were formed. These classes are:

(1) igneous rocks, which have solidified from molten material called magma;

(2) sedimentary rocks, those consisting of fragments derived from preexisting rocks or of materials precipitated from solutions; and

(3) metamorphic rocks, which have been derived from either igneous or sedimentary rocks. These three classes are subdivided into numerous groups and types based on various factors, the most important of which are chemical, mineralogical, and textural attributes.

The seven main minerals in rocks are Calcium, Phosphorus, Magnesium, Sodium, Potassium, Chloride, and Sulfur.

Crystals have several significant characteristics. Among these are the following:

Crystals are minerals that have gone through natural geological chemical processes and have solidified

Specific chemical compositions are unique to crystals

Crystals have an orderly geometric spatial pattern of atoms within their internal structures

There are 14 basic crystal lattice arrangements of atoms in the third dimension called *Bravais Lattices*.

Each lattice can be classified into one of seven crystal systems

Two minerals may have the same chemical structures but differ in their crystal structure. This condition is called a *Polymorph*. The crystals Pyrite and Marcasite are both iron sulfides but differ in their atomic structures. Another example is diamonds and graphite. Diamonds are viewed as the hardest of all minerals yet it has the same composition as the very malleable graphite.

Crystals and humankind's amorous fascination with them have been around for thousands of years. Their creation and use have been reported in early myths and legends. They were prominent in magic and the supernatural. For example, the Ancient Japanese creation myth has at its center a White Dragon whose breath created quartz. Quartz came to symbolize perfection. The Indigenous of Australia used Quartz to call for rain and it appears to be associated with maban, a mystical substance that provided the Kardjis their magical powers. Deucalion and Pyrrha, two survivors of the Great

Flood in Greek Mythology picked up 'stones' and threw them over their shoulders. These became the new race on Earth. The myth of the Chintamani in Tibet is a stone (crystal) that is said to be the grantor of wishes. The Ancient Celtics are said to have used 9 small clear quartz crystals placed in boiling water. Once cool, the water was drunk for 9 consecutive days. Today we talk about crystal elixirs.

Amber amulets have been found that are at least 30,000 years old. Amber beads dating 10,000 years old have been found in Great Britain. Paleolithic gravesites in Belgium and Switzerland contained Jet, a velvety black-colored gemstone that is a type of lignite. However, the first recorded use of crystals comes from the Ancient Sumerians in the fourth millennium, BCE. Two of their favorite crystals were Lapis Lazuli and Serpentine.

The Ancient Egyptians used Topaz and Peridot to combat night terrors and to remove evil spirits. The Egyptians also used ground crystals for cosmetics, especially Galena around the eyes.

China, Mexico, and South Americans used Jade masks for burial. It was also used to heal kidney issues. Malachite was another crystal used for cosmetic purposes. Additionally, Crystals also have had a role in the religions of the world: Hinduism, Buddhism, Muslim, and Christianity.

A shift in the belief in the use of crystals began in the early 17th Century when the physician to Rudolf II of Germany suggested that 'bad angels' tempted people believe in the crystals rather than God. Thomas Nicols in 1659 wrote Gemmarius Fidelius claimed crystals could not possess such effects as claimed in the past. The use of crystals for healing almost completely stopped during the 17th and 18th Centuries.

With the arrival of the 19th Century, there was a revival of interest in crystals. Experiments were conducted to demonstrate the effects crystals had on persons claiming to be clairvoyant. In 1880 two brothers, Pierre and Jack Curie found that heating and placing crystals under pressure created electricity. The effect is called the Piezoelectric Effect. The offshoot of this discovery has resulted in crystals being used in watches, sonar, inkjet printers, microphones, and many other products. However, it was not until the 20th Century and its "New Age Culture" that the use of crystals in healing re-emerged. On July 9, 1999, C. C. French and L. Williams presented a paper, *Crystal Clear:*

Paranormal powers, placebo, or priming? which detailed the use of crystals and healing at the Sixth European Congress of Psychology, Rome. Unfortunately, this paper was never published in a professional journal and as a consequence never received a peer review.

Despite the lack of significant scientific evidence, today crystals are used for the treatment of physical ailments such as burns, skin diseases, lung disease, hair loss, and cancer. They are used to help people with mental and emotional disorders. Critics claim any effect experienced by persons using crystals is simply the placebo effect. My attitude is if it works don't put it down.

CHAPTER TWO
CRYSTALS AND VIBRATIONS

Everything vibrates. The earth vibrates at 7.83Hz. A standing human being vibrates at 7.5Hz; whereas, when seated, the human body vibrates at a reduced 4.6HZ. The human body has 37.3 trillion cells. Imagine the movement, the vibration, the creation of healing energy going on.

A Hertz (Hz) is the number of cycles per second that any phenomenon goes through. Several decades ago, the Novel Laureate in Medicine, Albert Szent-Gyorgyi said "In every culture and every medical tradition before ours, healing was accomplished by moving energy. Our early healers who we have come to call *shamans* understood that sound created vibrations and those, in turn, created an energy that had a positive effect on their patients. These healers of old used drums, rattles, flutes, stomping feet, and voices to create sound.

Today we know that all things vibrate: Humans, animals, trees, plants, the earth, the universe-the cosmos itself. Cieda Uilye put it this way, "In the beginning, there were vibrations. And there was light, sound, and life."[i]

Albert Einstein once said, "Everything in life is vibration." But what is vibration? The definitions from the Oxford Dictionary of Languages are helpful.

"Vibration is an oscillation."
"Vibration is a person's emotional state, "

Cassandra Sturdy put it this way: "Your vibration is a fancy way of describing your overall state of being."

In the first Dictionary definition, vibration is said to be an oscillation. Is there a difference between vibration and oscillation? Yes. The main difference between oscillation, vibration, and simple harmonic motion is that oscillation refers to any repeated variation about a central value, while the term vibration refers specifically to mechanical oscillations.

In today's hectic world in which we are bombarded with serious climate change, worldwide pollution, daily violence, hate-mongering, heinous crimes against humanity, depletion of forests, and subsequent animal life create significant vibratory changes. These changes, all negative, impact every living thing including the cosmos itself.

Are there things you can do to increase your positive vibrations? Yes, there are. Several years ago I had the Reiki Principle "Just for today I will not be negative." A friend pointed out that the Principle itself was negative. She said to say "Just for Today I will be Positive." This is a good example of the first thing you should do. Examine your thinking processes. Are they primarily negative? Here is a short list of negative words. How many times a day do you use them?

Awful	can't	don't
gross	hate	
Icky	messy	no
not	never	
Stupid	sick	unfair
ugly	dumb	

In addition to examining your thoughts and actions, meditate Set a specific time every day to take ten minutes to meditate. Place some soft music, burn incense before you begin, and take a few Ocean Breaths. Immediately after your short meditation, say out loud 5 things for which you are grateful.

In1992, Bruce Taino built the world's first frequency monitor. Using his invention, Taino determined the Hertz of the human body to be 72 to 90. The human heart has a Hz between 67-70. Dr. Royal R. Rife found that certain frequencies could prevent and destroy certain diseases. Dr. Robert O. Becker has stated a person's health can be determined by the vibration frequency of the individual's body.

The question now becomes what can you do to positively change your vibrations to help heal yourself?

Crystals vibrate. Nothing spectacular about that statement since it is a fact that all things vibrate. What is it that crystals do? Here are 6 considerations:

1. Crystals, because of their vibration, increase the natural flow of one's physical energy, of one's life force
2. Crystals, sponge-like absorb negativity in your body; thus, they function as a cleanser.
3. Crystals work well in balancing one's energy centers called chakras
4. Crystal vibration induces healing
5. Crystals function as an aid to one's spiritual growth, and
6. Crystals help ground you or stabilize your emotional baggage.

CARING FOR YOUR CRYSTALS

Like any other physical thing, crystals have to be cared for. Just leaving them lying around is counterproductive. They gather dust, and negativity, and have their effectiveness drained. Here's what you can do to care for your crystals:

1. Wash your crystals in slightly warm water. Do not use any form of soap or cleaning liquids. Lay them out on a clean soft towel to dry

2. Place your crystals in a bowl containing sea salt. Leave them there for one hour, remove them from the bowl and gently brush off any remaining salt residue. Some users of crystals feel the salt may damage the crystals and weaken their strength

3. Place your crystal in the sun for one hour

4. Place your crystal in the moonlight overnight. Be sure your crystal is secure.

5. A saltwater bath is a good way to get rid of negativity. Mix 1 tablespoon of rock salt or sea salt in 1 cup of water. Make sure the crystals are fully submerged. Let them soak for 24 hours.

6. Brown rice is effective in drawing out negativity and other contaminants from your crystals. Depending on the number of crystals, fill a bowl with one cup of brown rice. Make sure the crystals are completely covered with the rice Let this stand for 24 hours. Discard the rice immediately after removing the crystals.

7. Sage, one of my favorite cleansers, is used to smudge crystals. To do a proper smudge you need the following: a fire-safe container, a lighter or match, and a bundle of dry sage. Light the sage,

select a crystal from the container, and hold it over the smoke from the sage. Do this for each crystal you want to be cleaned. Consider at least 15 seconds for each crystal.

8. Use a large Clear Quartz Crystal to clean smaller crystals. Place smaller crystals around the Clear Quartz. After 24 hours, remove the Quarz and place the clean crystals in a clean space. Gently rinse the Quartz in water and dry with a soft cloth.

HOW TO SELECT A CRYSTAL

How do you select a crystal? This question seems to plague many people. And it should not! The bottom line is if the crystal appeals to you, then buy it. But what if you feel the need to have more than just physical appeal as the basis for choosing a crystal? Consider the following:

First, select a crystal that attracts you by its color, shape, or size. Hold that crystal in the palm of your dominant hand. If you feel a slight vibration, and it will be slight, or if you feel a warmth from the crystal this then is the crystal you should accept and buy. Gently wrap your fingers around the crystal you are considering. If you feel a slight pulsing that's another sign you have the correct crystal. There is one other aspect of crystal selection and one that I feel is significant and that is intention.

Intention plays a significant role in all that you do whether you are aware of it or not. Intention sets the whole world of vibration into motion. The intention is what you desire and as long as that desire is not harmful to yourself or others, it will be honored. Your intention should always be specific. Don't say 'I want a new car.' Specific make, model, color, sedan, etc. With crystals, your intention for its use establishes its function. If it is to heal, heal what? Your intention should be in keeping with the crystal's natural properties.

Once you have your crystal, it should be programmed. This is such a simple thing to do. Unfortunately, many people forget it. Here are the steps to program your crystal.

PROGRAMMING YOUR CRYSTAL

The Steps:
1. Use a clean crystal
2. Write down your intention on a small piece of paper.
3. Use clear and concise language.
4. Fold the paper into a smaller piece
5. Place the folded paper into the palm of your dominant hand, but not tight
6. Sit in a comfortable chair or outdoors
7. Take 5 Ocean Breaths
8. Begin to meditate upon your intention. Say it as a mantra
9. Do this for 5 minutes.
10. Once you have completed this, place your crystal in a safe place.

Now that you have programmed your crystal it should be activated.

ACTIVATING YOUR CRYSTAL

1. In a secure spot (save from birds, animals, and children, place your crystal in the sun. Leave it there for 30 minutes.
2. Hold the crystal in your dominant hand, and spritz it with lavender hydrosol. Hold it for about two minutes and then gently wipe it dry.
3. Depending on the size of your crystal, place it in a dish filled with black pepper. The natural heat of the pepper will charge or activate the crystal. Leave in for an hour.

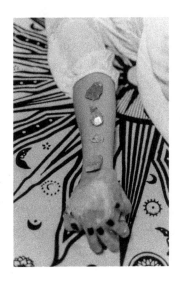

CHAPTER THREE
SPECIFIC HIGH VIBRATIONAL
CRYSTALS AND THEIR USES

A bit of biology is necessary here. Modern science tells us that cells are composed of molecules; each molecule is composed of atoms which in turn are composed of subatomic particles called protons, electrons, neutrons, and quarks. Additionally, according to engineers at Washington University, we know that there are about 100 trillion atoms in a single cell. Now, that's 12 zeros after the number 100. Furthermore, it is estimated that there are 100 billion cells in the human brain. All of these cells are in a constant state of vibration. Like everything else, crystals vibrate and in their natural environment, they connect to the vibration of the earth. As with all things in nature, there are positive and negative differences and there are highs and lows.

Let's begin with 8 crystals of high vibration: Benitoite, Blue Tourmaline, Creedite, Danburite, Goethite, Herkimer Diamond, Lemon Quartz, and Petalite.

Benitoite is a barium titanium silicate crystal that is found in rocks that have experienced hydrothermal metamorphism. That means changes that occurred in rocks that were near the surface where there was an intense activity of hot water. Benitoite is blue and has quiet energy. It is extremely rare and expensive; ranging from $6,500 to $8,000 for a piece 1 karat in size. Its claimed benefits include the following:

- Stimulates the expansion of joy
- Expands your consciousness
- Enhances the Third Eye Chakra
- Stimulates psychic abilities
- Increases awareness of synchronicity

Blue Tourmaline is composed of aluminum and borosilicate mixed with iron, magnesium, and other metals. Blue Tourmaline is rarer than the other Tourmalines. It comes in shades of light to dark blue. It is associated with the following benefits:

- Provides help in deep meditation
- Brings an inner peace
- Frees up the mind to explore higher consciousness
- Increase the ability to communicate honestly
- Increases the levels of intuition
- Amplifies clairvoyance, clairaudience, clairsentience.

One of the outstanding characteristics of Blue Tourmaline is its ability to become electrically charged. Simply, rub it with a clean hand. This is called pyroelectricity. Once charged, one end will be positive and the other negative. It will then attract small particles of dust.

Blue Tourmaline is a shaman's stone. It protects the shaman's work of rituals and healing sessions.

Creedite is another rare crystal. It is from the oxidation of Fluorite ore. It comes in a variety of colors: white, orange, purple, and even colorless. Creedite is a high-energy crystal. When paired with Black Tourmaline and Shungite it is significant as a grounding crystal and helps you from becoming overwhelmed. It also helps with the following:

- Enhances spiritual communication
- Helps ease connection to the Akashic Records
- Helps in interpreting messages from your Spirit Guides
- Helps clear any blockages in the higher Chakras
- Helps replenish your aura
- When combined with Moldavite it helps you to accept higher frequencies; thus, move to higher levels to develop you into all you can be.

Danburite is a mineral called calcium boron silicate. Its color ranges from white to a pale yellow and may show a touch of light brown. A cut Danburite crystal can cost somewhere in the neighborhood of $10,000. Originally discovered in 1839 in or around Danbury, Connecticut from which its name is derived. Danburite is high vibrational and because it is, it is credited with doing the following:

- Aligning the heart and crown chakras together
- Helps one to better process their emotions with a clarity
- Improves one's decision-making processes
- Helps to reduce stress
- Can help you to access higher knowledge as communication with your Spirit Guide improves.

As with many things, it will take time for you to become comfortable with the energy from Danburite. If you have difficulty even after many sessions of meditation, consider carrying one or more of these crystals: Hematite, Galena, Black Tourmaline, or Selenite. You may want to consider the following procedure to soften the Danburite energy flow:

1. Use a Selenite wand. Be sure it has been polished. Otherwise, you will have white residue all over your clothing.
2. Beginning at your shoulder, sweep the Selenite Wand down to the time of your fingers. Do this three times. Sweep both arms.
3. Do not apply pressure. Just be natural.
4. By the way, this is also an excellent way to eliminate negative energy.

Be patient if you use this crystal. It may take time to feel at ease with its energy. Meditate.

Goethite named after Johann Wolfgang von Goethe is an iron oxide-hydroxide mineral. Its colors range from red to black-brown. Its price ranges from $35 to $595. Known as a healing crystal, Goethite is said to generate a deep concern for the environment and to help you heal after the loss of a loved one. It is an excellent aid in the following areas:

- Grounding
- Metaphysical attributes such as helping you to connect with your Spirit Guides
- Writer's block
- Unleash your creativity
- Healing in the area of the ears, nose, and throat
- It is said it will soothe symptoms of epilepsy
- Boost the concentration of those who suffer from ADD
- Love is enhanced

Goethite is an excellent stone to work with other crystals; for example:

1. Boosts the energy of Smokey Quartz
2. Used with Pink Danburite or Pink Petalite will deepen your meditation
3. Combined with Sillimanite, Herkimer Diamond, or Blue Cavansite will enhance your clairaudient abilities
4. Used with Chiastolite, Lemurian Seed Crystal, or Miriam Stone will help you access the Akashic Records.

Herkimer Diamond Is not a diamond at all. It is a form of double-terminated quartz crystals that began forming 500 million years ago in the dolomite outcrops throughout Herkimer County, New Year, and the Mohawk River Valley from which its name is taken. The Herkimer Diamond is considered to be the most powerful of all the Quartz Crystals. And like its sister quartz crystals, it is a powerful healer. Among those areas in which it renders healing are the following:

1. Fights pain
2. Purifies the body of toxins
3. Helps the metabolic rate
4. Helps prevent physical burnout
5. Stimulates the immune system
6. Acts to attune to another person
7. Increases the energy of other crystals

Herkimer Diamonds are very useful in connecting to the higher spiritual domains by opening the potentiality for direct communication with your Spirit Guides. Additionally, the Herkimer Diamond is said to be a powerful tool for astral travel.

According to Cassandra Eason (The New Crystal Bible. London: Carlton Books, Ltd. 2010), Herkimer Diamonds are not for children or animals. Carrying Herkimer or wearing it as jewelry for long periods may cause disorientation for some individuals. As with all supportive medicines and treatments always check with your medical doctor.

Lemon Quarts is unique among crystals. It is man-made by heating yellow quartz, amethyst rock, and iron minerals together at very high temperatures somewhere around the 900-degree mark. It is a piezoelectric stone, that is, it can generate an electric charge.

Even though Lemon Quartz is quite a hard stone it should not be exposed to heat or direct sunlight because it may change its beautiful lemon color. It is a crystal that has metaphysical qualities. Among these qualities are the following:
- Connects to the brain and helps one to focus and to structure and enhance thought patterns
- Helps produce clarity
- Helps you make decisions
- Fights lethargy
- It will help stabilize your mood swings.

Cleansing lemon quartz crystals includes somewhat rather unique techniques including the following:
- Leave the lemon quartz crystal outdoors under a full moon all night. Make sure to retrieve it before sunrise. Also, make sure it is secure,
- Bury the lemon quartz crystal in your garden and leave it buried for 48 hours. Once retrieved, rinse with water,
- Smudge the crystal with sage or Palo Santo,

- Place the crystal in a small dish filled with Himalayan Salt for 12 hours,
- Place the Lemon Quartz Crystal next to a piece of Selenite. It will cleanse the stone and recharge it.

Petalite is the final crystal o be discussed in this group. It is a lithium aluminum silicate. Fine Petalite is rare. It is easily confused with Feldspar. Petalite's glassy appearance and its pearly luster are its distinguishing characteristics. It can be gray, white, green, yellow, pink, or reddish. It is very brittle and is seldom cur. Petalite has several physical and emotional attributes. These are as follows:
- Helps cut time with the past
- Supports personal independence
- Clears negative emotions and makes you less sensitive
- Enhances your compassion
- Promotes flexibility
- Energizes all the energy centers of the body, the chakras
- Benefits your eyes, lungs, and internal organs
- Reduces muscular spasms

ACTIVITY: Creating a Crystal Spray Cleanser
1. You will need a crystal of choice. For our example, I will use Lemon Quartz

2. You will also need the following: a clean sterilized glass jar and lid, distilled water, a spritzer, a piece of gauze, and a rubber band
3. Carefully place your crystal (no Selenite) in the jar
4. Pour the distilled water into the jar until it is just below the top
5. Cover the top of the jar with gauze, and secure it with the rubber band.
6. Set the bottle in a safe place, but not in the direct sunlight
7. Let this stand for 48 hours, then remove the gauze, and place the lid on the jar.
8. Refrigerate for 12 hours
9. Remove the lid, and carefully fill the spritzer.
10. Lightly spritz a counter, leather chair, table, or desk. Waite a few seconds and then wipe dry.

Creating a Crystal Grid

A crystal grid is simply an arrangement of attuned crystals placed in a sacred geometric shape that is charged by your intention. The crystals amplify each other. You should always have a specific intention for any crystal grid you create. Don't create a crystal grid just because it looks pretty or makes an attractive decoration.

Crystals have auras. Keep that in mind as you construct your grid. You will not want to use crystals whose auras may conflict.

You may create your grid to heal a family member, a friend, or yourself. You may create a healing grid for a pet or a plant.

You will need the following to create a crystal grid:
A safe place to lay out your crystals
15 to 30 crystals, each should be supportive of each other and your intention
One larger stone for the centerpiece
Three slightly smaller stones, preferably the same kind

I suggest a good-sized piece of Clear Quartz as the center stone, six smaller Clear Quartz crystals flowing outward from the center, and the remainder stones be amethyst. Some people also add a crystal ring around the outer edge of the grid. The outer stones help to amplify your intention to the Universe. Please note you can use whatever crystals you want.

Once your grid is constructed it is necessary to activate it. Use a selenite wand or your hand and if you don't have a wand place it directly over the grid and as you do visualize a warm flame passing over the grid. Say your intention out loud. Conclude by expressing your gratitude for the help and support of the grid.

Here is an example of a simple grid layout. Crystals have not been placed. Remember, you may create your grid in any shape, larger, or smaller with more or fewer crystals.

Crystal Grid for _____

Intention Statement: _____
_____
_____

CHAPTER FOUR
VIBRATION THERAPY AND CRYSTALS

In Module Two I discussed vibration, what it was, and how it was measured. There is, also, Vibration Therapy. It has been around as a concept since 1867 when Dr. Gustav Zander invented an apparatus that created a sense of vibration and used it for therapeutic purposes. Nearly three decades later in 1895, another doctor, John Harvey Kellogg, included vibration in his practice. During the early years of space exploration, Russian doctors realized that astronauts were experiencing considerable bone loss which was not normal for people their young age. In today's Space World, NASA uses vibration therapy to help prevent bone loss.

How does vibration therapy work? There are several hand-held vibration machines currently available as well as platform types. Vibrating machines may result in your body producing more osteoblasts.

Crystals, which produce a more subtle vibration than do the machines, never-the-less, offer therapeutic value not just in physical aches and pains but also in mental and emotional pains. Among the benefit claims are the following:
1.   Reduction of joint pain
2.   Improvement of circulation

3. Alleviates stress
4. Boosts metabolism.
5. Reduces muscle tremors
6. Calm emotional issues
7. Reduces depression

As with any of the suggestions, implied use of crystals or their byproducts, always check with your medical doctor before using any of these suggestions which are offered here only as supportive medicine and never as a replacement for modern medical practices.

Using Vibrational Therapy may be potentially dangerous for those individuals who suffer various physical and emotional issues. Your medical doctor may advise you to stay away from using vibrational machines and high vibrational crystals if you experience any of the following:
- Using blood thinners
- Have advanced diabetes
- Have heart issues
- Are pregnant

Today crystals are involved in nearly every aspect of our lives from cellphones to space satellites. Because crystals' structures are such that they have low entropy and because of that, they are responsive to and engage all the different energies surrounding them. Their balance and their frequencies certainly make them an important tool in healing. These crystals are high vibration stones and are excellent healers: Clear Quartz, Watermelon Tourmaline, Jade, Selenite, Celestite, Chalcedony, Shungite, Tanzanite, and Hematite.

Clear Quartz admittedly is one of my favorite crystals. Without a doubt, it is one of the world's most popular crystals. Its name comes from the Greek, krustallos, which means ice, and the German word, Quarz, meaning hard. It is used for the following:

- Increases your biomagnetic field
- Protects against radiation
- Dispels static electricity
- Generates electromagnetism
- Radiates all the color vibrations within the light spectrum
- Helps focus one's mind
- Harmonizes and balances universal energy
- Stimulates the immune system

ACTIVITY ONE: MAKING A HEALING BAG

If you are feeling disgruntled or mildly depressed make a healing bag. You will need the following:

- A sheet of gauze, scissors, needle, thread, and at least one piece of Clear Quartz.
- Make sure the crystal is clean, has been programmed, and activated.

- Cut the gauze into a four-inch square
- Place the clean crystal in the center of the square gauze
- Sew up the sides; leaving an opening for the crystal
- Tie off the top with a piece of string, ribbon, or rubber band
- Hold the gauze bag in your dominant hand, gently closing it.
- Place the crystal bag in a safe place outside for 2 hours.
- Retrieve the bag, remove the crystal and gently wash it with cool water.

Watermelon Tourmaline

Watermelon Tourmaline is composed of aluminum boron silicate and also contains elements such as iron, manganese, sodium, lithium, and potassium. Discovered in 1902 in Newry Maine but

Brazil is known to be the source of the finest quality Watermelon Tourmaline. There are several reasons why you should consider adding this crystal to your collection. Among these reasons are the following:

1. Works well as a cleanser for your heart chakra,
2. Acts as a balancing tool for your insecurities, strengthens your dreams, and may help bring them to reality,
3. Inspires and activates your creativity
4. Simulates your thinking outside of the box,
5. Acts as a shield of protection

In terms of your physical and emotional being Watermelon Tourmaline will help in the following areas:

- Boosts your immune system
- Helps control hyperactivity
- Calms your heart
- Relieves symptoms of hysteria and paranoia
- Helps the proper function of the endocrine system
- Brings a balance to the right and left hemispheres of the brain
- Helps reduce pain

Watermelon Tourmaline is an excellent crystal to have in your workplace. It helps protect you from the negativity generated by electronics. Place a couple of the Watermelon Tourmaline crystals in a small bag under your pillow to help you sleep. It works well with the following crystals:

1. Quartz
2. Howlite
3. Botswana Agate
4. Rainbow Quartz
5. Rutilated Quartz.

Jade. Two distinct minerals are commonly called Jade: First, nephrite, a calcium magnesium silicate; second, jadeite is made of sodium aluminum silicate.

Nephrite comes in various shades of green, yellow, black, brown, grey, and white; whereas, Jadeite in addition to green comes in black, brown, grey, lavender, orange, red, white, and yellow.

How do you know which jade you have? There is a simple test you can do. Take a hard object such as the tip of a ballpoint pen, and tap the jade. Nephrite will produce a sound; jadeite will not.

As a crystal of high esteem, Jade has been used for thousands of years by the Chinese, Egyptians, Aztecs, and the Maori of New Zealand.

Jade, either the Nephrite or Jadeite, functions as a crystal of harmony. In addition to harmony Jade aides, the following:

- Love and balance to your heart

- Promotes healing
- Provides emotional support
- Transforms negative energy into positive energy
- Helps cleanse spaces

Like other crystals, Jade needs to be cleaned and activated. Please note, that Jade does not store negative energy. It does collect dust and oils from being handled.

Gently wash your Jade crystal in slightly warm water. No soaps or detergents. Dry with a soft cloth. It's all a good idea to wash the crystal after first purchasing it.

Once the Jade Crystal has been washed and thoroughly dried, hold it in the palm of your hand, and gently close your fingers around the crystal but not tight. Say out loud your intention for the stone. Do so, three times. Place it next to a Selenite wand for 24 hours.

Selenite a crystallized form of gypsum is considered to be one of the top crystals used by crystal healers. It contains powerful energy and provides protection. Even though, at this time, there is no evidence to support any of the healing claims made for Selenite itself there is for its trace element. A trace element is a chemical found in very small amounts in all living things. In this case, the trace element is *selenium.*

Selenite has six other names it is called: Satin Spar, Desert Rose, Gypsum Flower Butterfly Selenite, Golden Phantom, and Disodium Selenite. It also comes in three distinct shapes: An hourglass which is used for grounding; a wand which is used to cleanse, and a tower which is used to create a protective shield. The main healing qualities of Selenite are as follows:

- Promotes inner peace
- Stimulate clarity
- Because it vibrates at a high frequency, it clears blockages
- Elevates one's spirituality
- Encourages your intuition
- Enhances your ability to manifest
- Opens communication with your Spirit Guides

As do all crystals, Selenite needs to be cleaned. It should not be put in water. It will dissolve. Here are five suggested ways to clean your Selenite crystal:

1. Smudge the crystal with white sage or Palo Santo
2. Place the Selenite in a bowl of salt and leave it for two hours
3. Use the vibration from a crystal or Tibetan bowl
4. Set the crystal in sunlight for 30 minutes

5. Place the crystal in the moonlight overnight

CHAPTER FIVE
VIBRATION THERAPY AND
CRYSTALS CONTINUED

We will continue with some of those crystals listed in Chapter 4: Chalcedony, Shungite, Tanzanite, Celestite, and add Super Seven. Chrysoprase, and Kyanite.

Chalcedony is also called Sard or Carnelian. Its colors include white, pink, gray-blue, and red. A chalcedony crystal is a form of Silica. It has a creamy white luster and is not quite transparent. Chalcedony has several excellent attributes. Among these are the following:

- Brings into alignment all three aspects of the human being: Mind, Body, and Spirit
- Nurtures human endeavors in the areas of spirituality, and creativity.
- Promotes stability in one's life
- Enhances the ability to communicate with the Spirit World
- Helps in controlling your emotions
- Supportive when engaging in new projects
- Promotes personal benevolence.

Each of the colored Chalcedony has its special contribution. Red Chalcedony, encourages persistence, stimulates blood circulation, and reduces hunger pangs. There is a cautionary note, however. Do not use this crystal for long periods because it may prevent the body's ability to absorb necessary nutrients.

Pink Chalcedony enhances wonderment and curiosity and promotes a beautiful inner peace.

Blue Chalcedony fosters creativity, opens the mind for the assimilation of new ideas and promotes optimism about the future, and aids the improvement of upper respiratory issues.

White Chalcedony encourages clear thinking while under pressure, supports being comfortable with others, and fosters tolerance.

Probably the most significant aspect of using Chalcedony is in helping you to focus on the spiritual world without neglecting your developing objectives.

Cleansing and charging your Chalcedony Crystals is easy. Just hold them under warm water for a couple of minutes to wash away dust and grime. To charge your crystal place it inside an Amethyst geode. If you do not have a geode a piece of Amethyst will work. Simply place your Chalcedony next to the Amethyst or if possible, place it on top of the Amethyst but make sure it will not fall off and become damaged.

Shungite is what is called a mineraloid because of its structure, therefore, it is not a crystal. Despite that technicality, it is included with crystals as are opal and obsidian. It has a long history of use as a healing stone. Typically black, Shungite can be a deep bronze. Shungite is primarily carbon and those that are made up of clusters of carbon are called *fullerenes.* What are the health benefits of Shungite? Even though there isn't scientific evidence that the following work, they are never-the-less believed to be true:

> Helps lessen insomnia
> Relieves pain
> Improves energy
> Acts as detoxification for the body
> Functions as a protector against electromagnetism
> Grounding
> Helps bring your spiritual body into the physical realm and thus enhance your well-being
> Helps release stress
> Works well as a stone for mediation
> Used as an antimicrobial

The following procedures can be used to cleanse and recharge your Shungite"

- Visualization Technique- Sit in a comfortable chair. Play some Solfeggio Frequencies, hold your Shungite in your cupped hands, create your intention (In this case it would be for the Shungite to cleanse itself.), Take 4 Ocean Breaths, and then pause. Wait 5 minutes, remove the Shungite and place it in a clean, safe place.

- A second cleansing technique also brings your breath into play. Hold the crystal in your dominant hand. Quiet your mind. Blow directly onto the crystal. Then in an outward sweeping motion, waver your other hand over the crystal. Do that five times.

Tanzanite is one of the varieties of the mineral called *zoisite*. It is believed to be one thousand times rarer than diamonds. It is said that Maasai herders found blue crystals in the hills of Tanzania while tending livestock in 1967. They notified the prospector, Manuel D'Souza. D'Souza registered claims with the government to begin mining. One of the things that make this stone so admired is that it is a trichoic stone. That simply means it reflects different colors across several spectrums. In this case, ranging from light blue to deep indigos and violets.

A pure blue Tanzanite crystal roughly costs $425 per carat. Lager stones begin at $650 per carat.

What then, does Tanzanite do? Among the claims of its value as a healing crystal are the following:

Stimulates the throat, third eye, and the crown chakras

Activates the psychic ability

Facilitates communications with the Spirit Worlds

Assists in personal transformation

Alleviates skin issues

Boosts the immune system

Releases emotional issues

As far as cleaning is concerned it is recommended that warm water and mild soap should be used to clean a Tanzanite crystal. Dry it with a soft cloth. However, I continue to not recommend using soap because soap tends to leave a fine film. As far as I am concerned, use mildly warm water only. Never use cleaners or cleaning sprays.

As with all crystals, you should charge your crystal and then activate it. Here are two approaches to charging the Tanzanite Crystal:

- Create a small crystal grid of clear quartz and selenite. Place the Tanzanite crystal in the center of the grid. Depending on the size you have chosen, place the quartz in the first ring and the selenite in the outer ring surrounding the center. Leave the grid for 24 hours. Remove the crystals and return them to their normal location.
- Place the Tanzanite on a small piece of soft cloth. Using a crystal bowl, play the bowl as

you hold it over the Tanzanite. Do this for about two minutes. I prefer an Indigo Crystal Bowl.

After your crystal has been charged, take a few minutes to activate it. Use a meditation with a specific intention in mind. Say the meditation as a mantra five times, leaving a five-second pause between each statement of your mantra.

<u>Super Seven</u> is a unique and fascinating crystal. It is considered a rare crystal with a high vibration. There appears to be only one mine in the world that provides authentic Super Seven Crystals. It is located in Brazil. However, two other small mines claim to be a source of this crystal: One in Brazil and one in India. Neither of these locations seems to have provided authentic Super Seven crystals. They lack a crystal.

This magical stone contains the following crystals:

Amethyst which is a stone of physical and emotional issues

Cacoxenite, a positive stone, opens spiritual endeavors

Smokey Quartz, a healing crystal, helps one's ability to stay focused

Clear Quartz, a healing crystal amplifies auras and the flow of energy

Rutilated Quartz is a stone of optimism and stability

Goethite helps in making clear decisions and balance between the positive and negative energies

Lepidocrocite enhances intellectual ability and helps align you with the Divine.

Super Seven, sometimes called Melody or Sacred Stone helps access the spirit realm, unlocks knowledge within that realm, attunes your energy to that of the Spirit World, and expands your consciousness.

It's reported that Super Seven contains the vibrations of all the included crystals and makes it a stone of high protection.

Kyanite is formed in metamorphic rocks and generally occurs as shards. Its deep cerulean blue makes it a beautiful crystal. It may be black, grey, or turquoise. It is a stone of healing, protection, and clarity. Some healers may suggest wearing a piece of Kyanite around the neck to help clear blockages in the throat chakra. In addition to helping with blockages, Kyanite helps with the following:

Promotes inner peace
Helps with sleep disorders
Relieves built-up emotional stress
Functions as a potent cleanser
Helps relieve inner sadness

There are several ways to use Kyanite Crystals. Among these are:

Wear as a neckpiece
Carry in your pocket
Place on your nightstand
Place at your desk

As a Shamanic Healer, I recommend pacing the Kyanite Crystal in your dominant hand. Close your eyes and do three or five deep Ocean Breaths. Feel which part of your body is reacting to the Kyanite. Move the crystal to that area. Leave it there until you sense it has done its work or should be moved to another location on your body.

In cleansing, Kyanite do not use any abrasive or chemical cleaning agent. Simply soak the crystal in warm water for a few minutes, remove and dry with a soft cloth.

Chrysoprase is a translucent variety of Chalcedony and has a color range from yellow-green to a beautiful apple green. It is found worldwide. With large deposits in Australia, it is often referred to as Australia Jade. Chrysoprase is a crystal that supports the following"

Helps develop poise and grace
Helps you recognize your inner beauty
Encourages self-expression
Builds mental dexterity
Promotes hope
Encourages fidelity in personal relationships
Helps heal the inner child

Chrysoprase not only brings universal energy into the physical body but as it does so, it detoxifies the body.

Celestite is a strontium sulfate mineral found inside certain geodes. Celestite is brittle and has tiny prismatic clear shards. Discovered in 1799 by A. G. Werner, these stones' pale blue color is associated with the divine and wisdom. Most of the stones currently sold come from Madagascar and tend to be more green than blue.

Celestite is an excellent stone for facilitating the following:

Grounding
Develops harmony
Helps to heal heart and mind issues
Elevates your consciousness
Works with the pituitary gland in producing serotonin
Energizes
Helps you focus

Helps open psychic abilities.

Because of its delicate nature care should be taken in cleansing the Celestite Crystal. I do not recommend cleansing this crystal with soap and water. Drying it could be a problem. Instead, smudge the crystal with White Mountain Sage or Palo Santo, and then do not seal the crystal in a plastic bag. Place in it a glass or wooden container. Or you may place it in a glass cabinet.

Once the Celestite is cleansed, charge it by placing it near an Amethyst crystal overnight. Activate it with a clear intention.

An additional benefit gained by using Celestite is to place a piece on your bedside table. It will help promote deep sleep and help you to remember your dreams. By the way, keep a small notepad on your bedside table to jot down significant points of your dream.

Remember, your vibrational pattern is the overt expression of who you are but it expresses something more important. It identifies what you are.

CHAPTER 6
TWO HOT CRYSTALS

MOLDAVITE
In the first module, Using Crystals, I said I would discuss Moldavite. I am adding Compo del Cielo Crystal. Both of these high-energy crystals have at least three things in common: Both are from meteorites. One hit earth 15 million years ago while the other landed 4200 to 4700 years ago. One landed in Europe; the other in South America.

Moldavite is silica rock and comes in dark green or blue-green color. It is glass that formed when the meteorite impacted the earth. It is also a form of Tektite, a small, pebble-like glassy object that has been melted by the meteorite's impact, and shot back up into our atmosphere. It then fell back to Earth because of gravity. These crystals often take on aerodynamic shapes as they partially melt on their return to Earth.

Moldavite brings high vibrational energy as well as an energetic spiritual quality. Archaeologists have found cutting tools and amulets made of Moldavite dating back to 25,000 BCE. In Eastern Europe and Czechoslovakia. It is true as, with other things, people experience Moldavite in different ways. One of the more common reactions, especially by those who experience Moldavite for the first time, is what is called Moldavite Flush. Holding a Moldavite crystal in the palm of their hand first-timers experience an intense warmth, a tingling sensation along the spine. Sometimes, light-headedness is what the novice experiences.

Moldavite's claimed healing qualities include the following:

Helps with cell growth

Strengthens your eyes

Helps transforms negative behaviors into positive ones

Encourages the release of negative energy

Stimulates your psychic abilities

Helps open communication with your Spirit Guides

Works in balancing all the chakras

Activating Moldavite

Because of the high energy level of Moldavite, you may have to demonstrate a bit more patience. First, to cleanse the crystal follow these steps:

- Thoroughly cleanse the Moldavite Crystal. Slowly wash the crystal in warm running water. If your tap water is chemically treated you may want to consider using distilled water.
- Dry the crystal with a soft cloth
- Place the crystal in the sun for one hour
- Place the Moldavite next to a piece of Selenite for 24 hours. Do not place the crystal in a plastic bag. Store the crystal on a small piece of soft cloth on a shelf.

Once the Moldavite has been cleansed do the following to activate it:

- First, think of what the primary role of the Moldavite Crystal is to be; physical healing, for example
- Create a specific intention as a mantra for the crystal
- Hold the Moldavite in your dominant hand
- Take three Ocean Breaths.

- Say to yourself or out loud your mantra
- Using your other hand, sweep outward over the crystal.

The Moldavite Crystal is now ready to go to work. But what if you don't want to set an intention for this powerful crystal? It is not necessary. You can choose to let the Moldavite and its energy guide you.

One of the unfortunate situations in today's world is the proliferation of fake stones. Buy your crystals only from a reputable gemologist. Check to see if the dealer had any complaints, and ask for references. Moldavite's mossy green color is unique. It will contain inclusions, and various textures and can be smooth or lumpy in parts.

CAMPO DEL CIELO CRYSTAL

Campo del Cielo has a fascinating history even though its exact time of hitting the earth is not known. It is believed to struck 4,000 to 6,000 years ago in Chaco Province, Argentina. The first known written record of Campo's existence was in 1576. As the story goes, an appointed Spanish governor, curious about local native rumors of large iron deposits that had fallen from the sky, sent out a military expedition. The expedition, under the command of Captain de Miraval, went to a brush-covered area aptly named Campo del Cielo which means Field of the Heaven. Captain de Miraval returned with a few pieces from a large massive iron chunk which he called *Meson de Fierro* (Large Table of Iron).

The Campo is a polycrystalline coarse octahedrite. It contains these minerals:
- Kamacite---a nickel alloy
- Taenite---a nickel alloy
- Troilite---a rare iron sulfide

Because of its high energy, the Campo Del Cielo gemstone can help with the following:

- Assist you in arriving at the full physical transformation of our existence
- Elevate your consciousness to new heights
- Give you an energy boost
- Clear the air of all negativity that may be impacting your decision-making processes
- Helps self-expression
- Brings mental, emotional, and physical healing
- Improve your competency
- Strengthens the immune system

Cleaning the Campo Del Cielo Crystal

- If your tap water is chemically treated, you may want to consider using distilled water to clean the Campo.
- Do not use a brush to clean the crystal

- Place the wet crystal on a soft cloth and let it air dry,
- Once the Campo is dry, place it in the sun for an hour
- Next place the crystal next to a piece of polished Selenite for 24 hours.

Activating the Campo Del Cielo

- First, think of what the primary role of the Moldavite Crystal is to be; emotional, for example
- Create a specific intention as a mantra for the crystal
- Hold the Campo Del Cielo in your dominant hand
- Take three Ocean Breaths.
- Say to yourself or out loud your mantra for this crystal
- Using your other hand, sweep outward over the crystal.

One further note: You can change the intention you set for any crystal. Just go through the cleansing and activating processes anytime you wish to change the intention of a crystal. Suppose you have a particular issue, a cut that won't heal, use your crystal but then you experience a deep sorrow of the loss of a loved one. You can use the same crystal by simply changing your intention for that particular crystal.

CHAPTER 7
CRYSTALS, ELIXIRS, FOOD, AND COSMETICS

Just a few years ago one would never think of adding crystals or gemstones as they are often called to drinks, foods, and cosmetics. Before I begin a very serious warning and a disclaimer. First, do your research and then double-check it. Some crystals are hazardous to your health. The following material is only suggestive and should not be used without first consulting your medical doctor.

First, a general warning about what crystals should not go in water: check the Mohs Hardness Scale and consider using only those crystals that have a 6 or higher rating. Second, avoid crystals high in iron ore and or copper. Third, take care in using crystals whose names end in -ite, for example, Malachite, Calcite, Hematite, Fluorite, and Selenite.

One of the frequently used crystal drinks is the elixir. What is an elixir? Unfortunately, the elixir is often confused with the word essence.

An **elixir** is defined as a medicinal potion comprised of water, alcohol, oil, or a combination of the three. An elixir can contain multiple essences.

Essence is the fundamental nature of things. It is the one thing or specific quality that defines the identifying character of a physical object. For instance, the essence of crystals is the vibration it generates.

When it comes down to a final answer, anything that is a derivative of water, oil, or alcohol and is enhanced with the vibration of a crystal is an Elixir. Others may not agree with me.

It is also necessary to remember all crystals are not safe to use. Here are 12 crystals that should NEVER be placed in your elixir water bottle or maker:
1. Amazonite
2. Angelite
3. Azurite
4. Chrysocolla

5. Garnet
6. Hematite
7. Labradorite
8. Lapis Lazuli
9. Malachite
10. Pyrite
11. Serpentine
12. Stibnite

All of these listed crystals contain copper, lead, sulfur, aluminum, iron, and fibrous material. These tend to build up in one's system and then create serious physical and emotional issues.

Five crystals are generally considered safe to use in the creation of an elixir: Amethyst, Black Obsidian, Carnelian, Citrine, and four quartz (Clear, Rose, Rutilated, and Smoky).

Crystal Elixir Bottles are available and range in price from $25 to $100. The pricier bottles have crystals encased in a separate glass container that screws into the bottom of the bottle. This can be changed out for different crystals. The less expensive bottles contain only one non-replaceable crystal.

CREATING YOUR CRYSTAL ELIXIRS

If you are a do-it-yourself type individual here is how to make a crystal elixir of your choosing. You will need the following:

MATERIALS:

> 1-quart glass bottle including its top, a pot large enough to hold the bottle and tap water, I quart of distilled water, a piece of gauze large enough to fit over the top of the glass bottle, a rubber band, a glass bowl large enough to hold the bottle. Two clear Quartz Crystals and two Amethyst Crystals, each about the size of a quarter.

DIRECTIONS: Set your intention before you begin.

1. Fill the pot with enough tap water to cover the glass bottle and its lid.

2. Carefully insert the bottle and its lid and bring the water to a full rolling boil. Reduce the heat to a gentle boil for 15 minutes to ensure their sterilization.

3. Slowly empty the pot of its boiling water. Be very careful. Remove the glass bottle and its lid. Set aside on a clean surface and let cool.

4. 1 quart of distilled water (If you are comfortable using tap water, do so)

> If you choose to use tap water boil it for 15 minutes.

5. Pour it into your glass bottle and let cool. Place a piece of gauze over the top and secure it with a rubber band.

6.   If you have opted to use distilled water, fill the glass bottle to the top and secure the lid.

7.   A bowl large enough to hold the quart bottle. Place the filled glass bottle in the center of the bowl. Fill the bowl with water.

8.   Carefully place the Clear Quartz Crystals and the Amethyst Crystals around the base of the glass jar.

9.   Let this sit, not in direct sunlight, for good 48 hours.

10.   Remove the glass bottle from the bowl. Remove the gauze and rubber band. Place the lid on the bottle, making sure it is on tight.

11.   Remove the crystals and rinse in warm water, dry with a soft cloth and return to a place of safekeeping.

12.   Empty the water from the glass bowl, wash and dry and put it away.

13.   Refrigerate the glass bottle overnight.

14.   Drink one ounce once a day. Make your elixir when it needs to be replenished.

In a hurry? Here's a shortcut. You will need a pan for boiling water, a stainless-steel slotted spoon, a sterilized glass bottle and lid, two to four crystals of your choice (keeping in mind the list of those crystals not to use), and a piece of gauze and a rubber band, a quart of distilled water.

DIRECTIONS:

In the clean pot, place the crystals, and add the distilled water. Place the pot over medium heat. As soon as the water begins to boil, remove the pot from the heat. Let this cool. Using the spoon, gently remove the crystals and place them in the glass bottle, add the water, and seal the top with the gauze and rubber band. Let sit overnight.

Remove the crystals, rinse and dry with a soft cloth. Refrigerate. Drink one ounce a day.

CREATING A FOOT OR BATH SOAK USING CRYSTALS

Once you have created a crystal elixir you can use the same base to create a wonderful foot soak or bath.

DIRECTIONS FOR A CRYSTAL ELIXIR FOOT SOAK

1. Use two ounces of your prepared crystal elixir. Warm it in a microwave or on top of a stove. Do not bring to boil or near-boiling.

2. Once the elixir is warmed add four to eight drops of your favorite essential oil. I suggest Rosemary Essential oil for the feet.

3. Pour the mixture into a pan large enough for your feet, and add warm water. Enjoy.

DIRECTIONS FOR A CRYSTAL ELIXIR BATH
1. Follow the procedures for the foot soak.
2. Place the elixir in the bathtub, and fill with the desired about of warm water.
3. I suggest using Lavender Essential oil if you are a woman; Cedarwood Essential Oil if you are a man.

MAKING A ROSE QUARTZ PINE NEEDLE TEA

Things you will need:
1. Four cups of Rose Quartz Crystal Elixir

2. Four drops of Lion's Mane Mushroom Extract
3. Pot or tea kettle for boiling water
4. Measuring cup
5. Teapot
6. Two to three cups of fresh pine needles
7. One to two teaspoons of raw honey
8. A cup and tea strainer
9. A spoon

Directions:

In the pot or tea kettle bring the four cups of Rose Quartz Crystal Elixir to a high boil.

Rinse the pine needles in the water. Pat dry and medium chop

Place the chopped pine needles into the teapot,

Carefully pour the hot Rose Quartz Crystal Elixir into the pot.

Let the tea steep for five minutes,

Pour the tea through the strainer into your cup. Add the honey and Lion's Mane Mushroom Extract. Stir. Enjoy.

A bit of information about Pine Trees. There are 115 different species of Pine Trees in the world. In North America, there are 36 species. The fresh needles of the Pine offer an excellent source of vitamins; especially C, E, A, and B. If you have an allergy, be sure to check with your medical doctor to see if you should have Pine Tree Needles. There is a growing body of evidence that Pine Needles help prevent cancer. Check out these two sources:

http://www.ncbi.nlm.gov/pmc/articles/PMC5776635

https://pubmed.ncbi.nlm.nih.gov/17474862/

AMETHYST ELIXIR REJUVENATION DRINK

There are several health benefits claimed by this drink. Among the more important benefits are the following:

- Lowers blood pressure
- Lowers high cholesterol levels
- Helps prevent the thinning of blood
- Prevents the hardening of blood vessels

You will need the following:

1, 8 ounces of Amethyst Elixir
2. 4 cloves of garlic finely chopped
3. juice of 5 lemons
4. 4 tablespoons of raw honey
5. Mixing bowl, knife, spoon, and glass jar

Directions:

Make the Amethyst Elixir

Chop the garlic, juice the lemons, and add the honey.

Thoroughly mix these ingredients and then add the Amethyst Elixir

Store in a glass jar with a lid. Keep refrigerated.

Take one teaspoon the first thing in the morning and one just before bed. Do this every day for one month.

CRYSTAL ELIXIRS AND BAKING

Some food recipes using crystals are beginning to appear in print. You should never consider using ground crystals (gemstones) in any kind of cooking. Check with your medical doctor before using any crystal elixir in your foods, beverages, on home cosmetics. With that said, one of my favorite snacks is Crystal Cocktail Zucchini Muffins. Because of the fifteen ingredients plus five crystals, the recipe will not be included here. It is available for your use and download in Resources.

Another outstanding crystal baking recipe is Blueberry Orange Muffins. The recipe and directions are available at this site:
> https://www.crystalvaults.com/blog/baking-with-crystals-bbobm/?utm_source=rss&utm_medium=rss&utm_campaign=baking-with-crystals-bbobm

CRYSTALS AND COSMETICS

The Ancient Egyptians are said to have used crystals cosmetically at least 10,000 years ago. They ground the crystals Galena and Malachite into fine powders and used them as an eye shadow or eyeliner. Kohl, as it was called has a soft texture and renders a silky finish. However, because Galena is lead-based I do not recommend using it. Lead, if used over a long time, can di irreplaceable physical harm. Lead is poisonous. However, several crystals are beneficial to your skin. Among these crystals are:

1. Amethyst aids skin sensitivities caused by stress
2. Quartz helps energize skin growth
3. Citrine provides a natural glow to the skin
4. Ruby helps the production of new skin cells
5. Diamond improves the radiance of the skin
6. Jade is used as a facial and helps soothe the skin

There are ready-made cosmetics that use crystals. However, for those who prefer to make their crystal skin cream a couple of recipes are included here.

Creating Lip Balm
  What you will need:
1. A sterilized small jar with a lid,
2. One of the following base oils: beeswax, sweet Almond Oil, or Hempseed Oil,
3. Lavender Essential Oil or one of your own choice. Just remember not all essential oils are appropriate for the skin.
4. A mixing bowl and a whisk
5. Amethyst Crystal Elixir

<u>Directions</u>:

While the jar and lid are being sterilized, take 2 ounces of the base oil of your choice, two drops of Lavender Essential Oil, and two drops of Amethyst Crystal Elixir. Mix until blended. DO NOT exceed the amount of Essential Oil or Elixir.

Carefully remove the jar and lid from the boiling water, cool, and thoroughly dry.

Add the mixture to the jar and place the lid. To provide an extra touch, place the jar in the refrigerator for a couple of hours. Makes a great refresher on a hot summer's day.

One more example of crystals used cosmetically will end this module. Men are now getting very much involved in skin care. One area of concern is the face.

Making A Facial Mask

<u>What you will need:</u>
1. A mixing bowl
2. A fork or whisk
3. A ripe avocado
4. Raw Honey
5. Unflavored yogurt
6. Lavender Essential Oil or oil of choice

<u>Directions:</u>
Peel the avocado, remove the seed Remove 2 ounces and set the remainder aside,

Place the 2 ounces of avocado into the mixing bowl. Add 1 tablespoon of raw honey, 2 tablespoons of unflavored yogurt, and 3 drops of Lavender Essential Oil. Whisk until thoroughly mixed.

Gently apply it to your face and leave it on for 10 to 15 minutes. If you are comfortable with the application, you can add 5 minutes. Rinse with warm water, and pat your face dry.

If you are a man and want to use an oil different than Lavender, consider Cedar Essential Oil.

A continued reminder to always check with your medical doctor before trying any of these suggested procedures. If you have skin issues check with your dermatologist.

CHAPTER EIGHT
CRYSTALS, ESSENTIAL OILS, AND
THEIR COMBINED USES

Logically, two natural healers should be married and create a more powerful healing potentiality. Adding crystals to an essential oil works when the correct pairing is done. Crystals and essential oils have some things in common:

1. Both are earthbound, that is, they are taken from the earth (Exception: meteorites)
2. Both have been used for healing and ceremonial purposes for several thousand years
3. Both are used to heal emotional, mental, and physical issues
4. Both enhance or strengthen each other's healing energies

Early on I described a crystal as "a solid that has an organized structure of a natural geometrically regular form with symmetrically arranged planes." The bottom line is crystals are minerals. What then, is an essential oil?

Essential oil is a compound that has been extracted from plants. This extraction captures the flavor of the plant or its "essence". Each oil has a distinctive odor. Essential oils are not taken internally. They are applied to the skin or inhaled via a diffuser.

Using crystals with essential oils is synergistic. Synergistic is the relationship of interactions or the cooperation of two or more substances to produce an effect greater than their separate effects. There are specific based steps to bring about the marriage of crystals and their complementary essential oils.

STEPS IN SELECTING CRYSTALS AND THEIR COMPLEMENTARY OILS

1. Accept the crystal that attracts you either by its color, shape, or feel.
2. Research your selected crystal: What are its chief characteristics? What areas does it provide healing and or protection?
3. Select an Essential Oil: Research your selection. Does the oil have similar healing qualities as your chosen crystal? More will be said of Essential Oils in a later course, but for now, make sure you get high-quality pure oil.
It is generally not recommended that one place pure essential oil directly on the skin. Therefore, you should consider a base oil: Jojoba, Macadamia, or Sweet Almond Oil.

All too often people just throw the crystal and Essential Oil together and then are disappointed because the combo didn't do anything. And therein lies the rub. You need to set the intention-your intention for the crystal/oil combo. Suppose you have chosen amethyst and paired it with Lavender Essential Oil because you want to lessen the stress you are feeling. Here are the steps for setting the intention for your amethyst and lavender combo:

1. Identify what you want the crystal and its paired lavender essential oil to do. Be specific. For example, say "Lessen my stress" three times as you hold the crystal in one hand and the essential oil in your other hand. Do this three times a day for three days.
2. Mix two drops of lavender essential oil with three drops of base oil.
3. Pour the oils into a small bottle, and add amethyst crystal chips. Mix well.
4. Let this rest for a full 24 hours.
5. Apply a small amount to each of your temples.

One of the major goals of all healing therapies is the promotion of positivity. An upbeat side effect of this positive energy is the development of a sense of calm. You can develop and promote this important health quality by using crystals and essential oils. You can buy small packs of already crushed crystals. Do not attempt crushing your own.

What You Will Need:

   ¼ to ½ teaspoon of crushed Citrine

   1 oz of Ylang-ylang Essential Oil

   2 oz of base oil (for this I suggest Jojoba)

   A small bottle with a roll-on top (A regular screw on top is acceptable)

Directions:

1. Mix the Citrine, Ylang-ylang and Jojoba oil
2. Remove the roller from the bottle and pour in the mixture. Replace the roll-on cap.
3. Hold the bottle in your dominant hand for a couple of minutes.
4. Using the roll-on, apply twice to one wrist and then gently rub both wrists together a couple of times.

Alternative:

   If you do not have a roll-on type bottle a regular small bottle will work just as well. Carry the non-roll-on bottle in a pocket or securely wrap a small chain around the bottle and wear it around your neck.

There are many life-enriching uses for combining crystals and essential oils. Here are a few examples:

   1. Protection from Negativity

   People often ask what can they do to protect themselves from negativity from others, the environment, and from within themselves. A crystal-oil combination that is often suggested is a combination of Black Tourmaline and Frankincense. Follow the procedure listed above. By the way, if you experience a negative work environment, place a Black Tourmaline Crystal on your desk. This suggested combo works well in a diffuser. Just make sure none of the crushed Black Tourmaline gets into the diffuser.

2. Building Self-Confidence

Most of us at some point in our busy lives experience a loss of self-confidence. It happens before an important business presentation, giving a talk at a local charity, changing job locations, buying a house, or any number of other daily situations. A combination of Rose Quartz and Bergamot Essential Oil works wonders in helping to restore your self-confidence. Because Bergamot Essential Oil is quite strong, you may want to reduce the amount used, for example, use ½ ounce instead of a full ounce.

3. Manifest Health and Happiness

The concept of manifesting has been around for several years. We often ignore and then forget some of the little signs that all is not as it should be in our daily lives and that includes general well-being. Well-being implies good health and overall happiness. To help reinforce both of these desirable qualities consider these crystal essential oil combinations:

1/3 ounce of crushed Pyrite Crystal
½ ounce of Cardamom Essential Oil

¼ ounce of base oil (I have deliberately suggested less base oil to up the positive effect of the essential oil.)

1/3 ounce of Bloodstone
1/3 ounce of Ylang-ylang Essential Oil
1/3 base oil

4. Connecting to Your Higher Self

The phrase "your higher self" has been and is tossed around more often than a basketball in a basketball game. Frankly, it is simply that part o you that has not been messed up by the ego and all the discriminations it creates. The question now is, are there things you can do to help you connect to that unencumbered you? From my perspective there certainly is. Clear Quartz immediately comes to mind. It becomes even more powerful when married to Clary Sage Essential Oil or White Sage Essential Oil. Both sages are powerful. Here's the recipe for Clear Quartz and Sage Essential Oil combination:

RECIPE FOR CONNECTION TO YOUR HIGHER SELF
You Will Need

½ ounce of crushed Clear Quartz Crystal
¼ ounce of Clary or White Sage Essential Oil
1 ounce of base oil (If you have no nut allergies try Almond or Macadamia Oil otherwise use Jojoba Oil.
A clean and sterilized small bottle with a cap or roll-on

Directions:
Place the oils in the bottle, replace the top
Shake to make sure the oils are well mixed
Place one or two drops at the Third Eye

Be patient with this one. It sometimes takes time and several applications. Apply the mixture at bedtime. If you have any negative reactions immediately stop using. Check with your medical doctor.

5. Heart Healing
In today's angst-filled world the human heart is placed under a great deal of emotional and physical stress. Unfortunately, and all too often serious issues arise. As a helpful preventive consider a combo of Green Aventurine and Patchouli Essential Oil. Green Aventurine is an excellent crystal to use as a heart healer and to

clear and activate the Heart Chakra. It is good for general well-being and emotional calm. Patchouli Essential Oil helps ground you, lessens your stress levels, and thus helps the heart.

RECIPE FOR HEART HEALING
<u>You Will Need</u>

¼ ounce of Green Aventurine Crystal chips
½ tablespoon of Patchouli Essential Oil

<u>Directions</u>
Combine these ingredients,
Add them to your bottle
Shake the bottle to make sure the ingredients are well mixed

Gently apply a small amount to your forehead.

CHAPTER NINE
CRYSTAL THERAPY FOR
DEHYDRATION ISSUES

Roughly sixty percent of adult men's bodies are water. It is a fact that fat tissue does not have as much water as lean tissue. Adult women have more fat tissues and as a consequence, only 55 % of their bodies are made of water. Working out, doing yard work, or other physical tasks leaves the body lacking water. This is dehydration. When you are absorbed in working out or doing other physical activities, it is all too easy to become dehydrated.

There are many symptoms of dehydration. Thirst is not always an early sign you need water. It is extremely important to be aware of the following symptoms in babies:

- Dry mouth as well as a dry tongue
- Lack of tears even when crying
- Sunken eyes
- Indented soft spot at the top of the skull
- Irritability

Symptoms of dehydration in adults include the following:

- Extreme thirst
- Infrequent urination
- Urine is dark

- Sudden fatigue
- Sudden bouts of Dizziness
- Periods of confusion

Besides not drinking enough water there are other causes of dehydration. Among these are:

- Severe diarrhea
- Heavy vomiting
- High fever
- Excessive urination
- Extreme sweating

Dehydration can cause serious emotional and physical issues even death. Among the issues that may be caused by dehydration are the following:

- Depression
- Increases bodily stress
- Anxiety
- Panic Attacks
- Hypovolemic shock
- Heart attach
- Kidney failure
- Seizures

What can you do to help safeguard against becoming dehydrated? First, ensure you drink enough water; not soft drinks, teas, coffee, or alcoholic beverages. Some authorities in the field suggest that women should drink about 92 oz of water per day and men 124 ounces of water. What do you do if that amount of water is not always readily available for your use? I suggest using cool crystals as a supportive approach, especially during very warm summers. The following 9 crystals are recommended:

1. Agate---boosts one's overall energy and corrects electrolytes concentration
2. Jasper---helps relieve stress and abdominal pain and boosts the stamina of the user
3. Amazonite--helps increase the body's retention of water
4. Blue Topaz---works to help reduce dehydration saliva and incessant thirst
5. Moonstone--- in addition to being helpful to those suffering skin issues, it boosts your ability to seal liquids within your body. By the way, wear or carry the Moonstone beneath your clothing to avoid it being in direct contact with sunlight
6. Hematite---is an excellent antidote for chronic dehydration. Carry or wear it on your person. If you suffer anemia and lack of hydration Hematite is an excellent crystal
7. Citrine---blocks thirst and is an excellent crystal to help increase your body's capacity to absorb water
8. Heliolite---provides a radiant shield to protect you against dehydration; regulates body fluids and minerals in your body

9. Garnet---helps the natural distribution of energy, particularly during the summer and winter months

Each of these nine crystals can be worn as jewelry and can be made into elixirs. Remember, be cautious when using crystals ending in -ite. Use the standard method for creating a crystal elixir. If you prefer neither of these two, you have a third option and that is to carry the crystal in a pocket of your clothing, place several small pieces in a cloth bag and store it under your pillow, or put the crystal in a small dish and place it on your nightstand.

Stay hydrated during the heat of the day.

CHAPTER TEN
Crystals, Essential Oils and Their Uses©

Logically, two natural healers should be married to create a more powerful healing potential. Adding crystals to an essential oil works when the correct pairing is done. Crystals and essential oils have some things in common:

1. Both are earthbound, that is, they are taken from the earth (Exception: meteorites)
2. Both have been used for healing and ceremonial purposes for several thousand years
3. Both are used to heal emotional, mental, and physical issues
4. Both enhance or strengthen each other's healing energies

Early on I described a crystal as "a solid that has an organized structure of a natural geometrically regular form with symmetrically arranged planes." The bottom line is crystals are minerals. What then, is an essential oil?

Essential oil is a compound that has been extracted from plants. This extraction captures the flavor of the plant or its "essence". Each oil has a distinctive odor. Essential oils are not taken internally. They are applied to the skin or inhaled via a diffuser.

Using crystals with essential oils is synergistic. Synergistic is the relationship of interactions or the cooperation of two or more substances to produce an effect greater than their separate effects. There are specific based steps to bring about the marriage of crystals and their complementary essential oils.

STEPS IN SELECTING CRYSTALS AND THEIR COMPLEMENTARY OILS

1. Accept the crystal that attracts you either by its color, shape, or feel.
2. Research your selected crystal: What are its chief characteristics? What areas does it provide healing and or protection?
3. Select an Essential Oil: Research your selection. Does the oil have similar healing qualities as your chosen crystal? More will be said of Essential Oils in a later course, but for now, make sure you get high-quality pure oil.

   It is generally not recommended that one place pure essential oil directly on the skin. Therefore, you should consider a base oil: Jojoba, Macadamia, or Sweet Almond Oil.

All too often people just throw the crystal and Essential Oil together and then are disappointed because the combo didn't do anything. And therein lies the rub. You need to set the intention-your intention for the crystal/oil combo. Suppose you have chosen amethyst and paired it with Lavender Essential Oil because you want to lessen the stress you are feeling. Here are the steps for setting the intention for your amethyst and lavender combo:

1. Identify what you want the crystal and its paired lavender essential oil to do. Be specific. For example, say "Lessen my stress" three times as you hold the crystal in one hand and the essential oil in your other hand. Do this three times a day for three days.
2. Mix two drops of lavender essential oil with three drops of base oil.
3. Pour the oils into a small bottle, and add amethyst crystal chips. Mix well.
4. Let this rest for a full 24 hours.
5. Apply a small amount to each of your temples.

One of the major goals of all healing therapies is the promotion of positivity. An upbeat side effect of this positive energy is the development of a sense of calm. You can develop and promote this important health quality by using crystals and essential oils. You can buy small packs of already crushed crystals. Do not attempt crushing your own.

What You Will Need:
¼ to ½ teaspoon of crushed Citrine

1 oz of Ylang-ylang Essential Oil

2 oz of base oil (for this I suggest Jojoba)

A small bottle with a roll-on top (A regular screw on top is acceptable)

Directions:

1. Mix the Citrine, Ylang-ylang and Jojoba oil
2. Remove the roller from the bottle and pour in the mixture. Replace the roll-on cap.
3. Hold the bottle in your dominant hand for a couple of minutes.
4. Using the roll-on, apply twice to one wrist and then gently rub both wrists together a couple of times.

Alternative:

If you do not have a roll-on type bottle a regular small bottle will work just as well. Carry the non-roll-on bottle in a pocket or securely wrap a small chain around the bottle and wear it around your neck.

There are many life-enriching uses for combining crystals and essential oils. Here are a few examples:

1. Protection from Negativity

People often ask what they can do to protect themselves from negativity from others, the environment, and within themselves. A crystal-oil combination that is often suggested is a combination of Black Tourmaline and Frankincense. Follow the procedure listed above. By the way, if you experience a negative work environment, place a Black Tourmaline Crystal on your desk. This suggested combo works well in a diffuser. Just make sure none of the crushed Black Tourmaline gets into the diffuser.

2. Building Self-Confidence

Most of us at some point in our busy lives experience a loss of self-confidence. It happens before an important business presentation, giving a talk at a local charity, changing job locations, buying a house, or any number of other daily situations. A combination of Rose Quartz and Bergamot Essential Oil works wonders in helping to restore your self-confidence. Because Bergamot Essential Oil is quite strong, you may want to reduce the amount used, for example, use ½ ounce instead of a full ounce.

3. Manifest Health and Happiness

The concept of manifesting has been around for several years. We often ignore and then forget some of the little signs that all is not as it should be in our daily lives, including general well-being. Well-being implies good health and overall happiness. To help reinforce both of these desirable qualities consider these crystal essential oil combinations:

1/3 ounce of crushed Pyrite Crystal
½ ounce of Cardamom Essential Oil

¼ ounce of base oil (I have deliberately suggested less base oil to up the positive effect of the essential oil.)

1/3 ounce of Bloodstone

1/3 ounce of Ylang-ylang Essential Oil

1/3 base oil

4. Connecting to Your Higher Self

The phrase "your higher self" has been and is tossed around more often than a basketball in a basketball game. Frankly, it is simply that part o you that has not been messed up by the ego and all the discriminations it creates. The question now is, are there things you can do to help you connect to that unencumbered you? From my perspective there certainly is. Clear Quartz immediately comes to mind. It becomes even more powerful when married to Clary Sage Essential Oil or White Sage Essential Oil. Both sages are powerful. Here's the recipe for Clear Quartz and Sage Essential Oil combination:

½ ounce of crushed Clear Quartz Crystal

¼ ounce of Clary or White Sage Essential Oil

1 ounce of base oil (If you have no nut allergies try Almond or Macadamia Oil otherwise use Jojoba Oil.

Place one or two drops at the Third Eye Be patient with this one. It sometimes takes time and several applications. Apply the mixture at bedtime.

5.   Heart Healing

In today's angst-filled world the human heart is placed under a great deal of emotional and physical stress. Unfortunately, and all too often serious issues arise. As a helpful preventive consider a combo of Green Aventurine and Patchouli Essential Oil.

Green Aventurine is an excellent crystal to use as a heart healer and to clear and activate the Heart Chakra. It is good for general well-being and emotional calm. Patchouli Essential Oil helps ground you, lessens your stress levels, and thus helps the heart. Here's the recipe:
¼ ounce of Green Aventurine Crystal chips
½ tablespoon of Patchouli Essential Oil
Combine these, add them to your bottle
Gently apply to your forehead.

ALSO, BY NORMAN W WILSON, PhD

Butterflies and All That Jazz with Drs. James G
Massey and James A Powell
Windows and Images: An Introduction to the
Humanities with Drs. James G Massey and James A
Powell.
The Humanities: Contemporary Images
Shamanism: What It's All About
So You Think You Want to Be a Buddhist?
Promethean Necessity and Its Implications for
Humanity
DUH! The American Educational Disaster
The Sayings of Esaugetuh: The Master of Breath
A Shaman's Journey Revealed Through Poetry with
Gavriel Navarro
The Shaman's Quest
The Shaman's Transformation
The Shaman's War
The Shaman's Genesis
The Shaman's Revelations
The Making of a Shaman
Activating Your Spirit Guides
Healing-The Shaman's Way
How to Make Moral and Ethical Decisions: A
Guide
Teas Soups and Salads
Reiki: The Instructor's Manual
Shamanic Healing

UDEMY COURSES AVAILABLE

www.udemy.com

Healing-The Shaman's Way is a 17 video lecture program detailing healing techniques, use of sound, crystals, essential oils and herbs.

Healing-The Shaman's Way Crystals explores the world of crystals, their composition, enegy, and uses in healing processes. Included are recipes for elixirs, cosmetics, and food that are made with crystals.

CPSIA information can be obtained
at www.ICGtesting.com
Printed in the USA
BVHW050246311222
655320BV00003B/118

9 781786 958143